Elementary Cloudwatching

31 Meditations on Living without Time

Robert Wolfe

Karina Library Press
Ojai, California
2013

Karina Library Press
Discover the Unexpected

Elementary Cloudwatching: 31 Meditations on Living without Time
ISBN-13: 978-1-937902-18-6 (hardcover edition)

Karina Library Press
PO Box 35
Ojai, California 93024

www.karinalibrary.com

preface overleaf image, artwork by Robert Wolfe

Also by Robert Wolfe

Living Nonduality: Enlightenment Teachings of Self-Realization

The Gospel of Thomas: The Enlightenment Teachings of Jesus

One Essence: The Nondual Clarity of an Ancient Zen Poem

Science of the Sages: Scientists Encountering Nonduality from Quantum Physics to Cosmology to Consciousness

Always—Only—One: A Dialogue with the Essence of Nondual India

www.livingnonduality.org

*With gratitude to my publisher,
Michael Lommel*

Meditations

Preface	7
Where I Am Not	9
Framing the Question	11
Savage Country	15
The Empty Page	17
A Wayfarer's Reverie	19
Self as Time	23
Worldly Citizenship	25
Seeking Change	29
One Day, at a Time	31
The I-deal	35
News from the Ravine	39
Vacating the Mind	43
Sunday Matinee	47
No Reason	51
The Open Mind	55
Unexpected	59
Uncontrolled	63
Vulnerable	65
Take No Thought	69
Post Meridiem	71
Sufficient Unto The Day…	75
Morning After	77
Inseparable	79
Bring On The Clowns	83
Time is Comparison	89
The Black Period	91
The Beat Goes On	95
Nothing Special	99
As Is	103
Transit	107
Live It	111

Preface

This contemplative journal was composed over a period of about a year. The following entries have also appeared among the collection of monographs published as *Living Nonduality*: Framing the Question, The Beat Goes On, The Black Period, Where I am Not.

Robert Wolfe
Ojai, California

Where I Am Not

Mid-morning, after a light, early rainfall. It is cool, this late September day, but not at all cold. Surrounded, mostly, by redwoods, sunlight scatters through in places on the ground. A few insects are on wing, in this clearing; one in particular, a moth or a butterfly in the distance, seems ecstatically happy. A sole pigeon is out of eyesight in a cascara tree, but the fluttering of wings can be heard as it browses among the thinning leaves for those favored cascara berries. A slight movement of the breeze shakes loose—from leaves and needles—those raindrops reluctant to join the earth; some of the yellowed leaves plunge, freeform, with them.

The clouds are an attraction. They were at first daubs of gray against the light blue background. They moved toward my left, nearly as slowly as the minute hand on a clock. And, throughout, they maintained their integrity, without changing form as clouds seem usually to do. Beneath them, a slight film of wispy cloud moved, more quickly, in the contrary direction. Soon, this lower strata had disappeared. And, to my surprise, the daubs of clouds were moving now toward my right; they had become looser, cottony, and seemed to want to conjugate with each other, as clouds so often do.

They are not under control, in any meaningful pattern as we would define it. Their movements are not to be predicted. In that, partially, is their beauty. They are not intent on any particular thing, changing their direction to meet changes in the circumstances around them.

World peace is here. I ask myself why it happens to be in this particular spot—but not, according to the newspapers, in the rest of the world. There's the same blue sky. The same stuff that all clouds are made of. Tall, silent trees doing exactly what trees do everywhere. The sounds of birds and bugs going about their daytime work as if it were their coffee break. There is the dampened brown earth, with some ants in sunlight, some not. There is a human, sitting quietly in a canvas chair in this clearing, watching a cloud that is moving in two directions, away from its center, in the same moment.

There is peace in this solitary spot on the globe because, basically, there is "no one" here. The human, who is merely part of the landscape, has no agenda, no ideas, no intent or motivation; he will not be rising from his chair in a moment to attempt to control something, to influence or change anything. Where could he begin to make any changes that would lastingly improve on the situation?

This morning air, now, could not smell more delightful.

Framing the Question

I arrive at the home of John L., whom I have been told by the Hospice staff is dying of cancer, and I go into his bedroom to meet him. As I shake his bony hand, he looks up at me from the dark wells of his eyes: "I've seen you before." His voice is high-pitched and nasal, and he seems to be toothless.

"Very possible," I say. "I've lived here for twenty years. How long have you been in the area?"

His eyes focus on his wife, who is standing by my side. "I can't remember. How long have we lived here?"

"Nine years."

"Yes, it's very possible that we've met," I repeat. He and I continue to scrutinize each other. Aside from the thin, long form under the quilt, all I can see is his head and one pale arm. Thin hair, sunken eyes, an aquiline nose, a bristly beard. No, he is not someone that I recall having seen before.

Over the next few days, in a couple of brief visits, I get to know him a little better. And on the third occasion, I am alone with him for a couple of hours while his wife catches up on some grocery shopping. I sit by his bed, hold his glass of Dr. Pepper so he can drink it through a straw, and let him know that I am there to listen to him if he wishes to talk. But he is mostly monosyllabic, and gruff in a covertly amiable way. Considering his physique, appearance, and mannerisms, I would cast him (if I were directing the play) as a crusty goldminer.

Prominently on the wall of his living room are displayed framed scale drawings of a Swedish-made sailboat with beautifully flowing lines; not just a photograph of it, mind you, but a scale drawing showing even its inward detail. Next to it is an expensive sheath knife with his name engraved on the blade, the kind of thing only a skipper could wear on his belt in earnest today.

"You sailed?" I ask.

"Every weekend."

"I've never sailed. I have no idea what it's like."

"Nearest thing to heaven you'll ever get, my boy!"

He dozes off. I make a cup of coffee in the microwave and wander around the living room. Toward a rear corner, on one wall, is a collection of about a dozen family snapshots which have been matted and framed. A few of the pictures are of his daughter at various ages, and his son. But there are about three pictures I find myself lingering over, returning again from one to another. They are pictures of him and his wife. The first one was taken at their wedding forty-one years ago; it was a second marriage for both, and she is wearing a corsage and he is in a suit; he looks like he is in his thirties, tall, lean, sensitive, like a businessman on his way up.

The latest picture is in color, and I recognize his wife, at his side, so instantly that I suspect this picture was taken only a few years ago. The man is much taller than his wife, wearing a sport shirt and an easy smile; he looks vigorous but relaxed. I can picture this man as the skipper of a sailboat, a casual hand on the rudder, squinting confidently into the sea breeze, the wind tousling his hair.

I can picture him inviting me into their comfortable dual-wide in this mobile-home retirement park, asking me if white wine is okay, and then sitting back crosslegged in the easy chair to tell me all the things I don't know about how finely the Germans craft steel blades, his voice deep but warm.

Later, while out for my evening walk, I am struck by the fact that if I had known that man as I sense him in the photograph, there is no connection I would have made with the man I know in the deathbed. They may be the same height, but that is a different body in the deathbed; and my guess is that their personal ambiance is at least as different.

What became of the man in the photograph?: it is obvious to me that he is gone, has left this earth. We like to think in terms of continuity, that the other man somehow became this man. Could this man, even if he regained his health, ever again become the other man? No.

No, somewhere moment by moment the other man disappeared. The evidence we have that he existed is a photograph, a knife, a blueprint. The man in the bed, though still alive, has already let go—even if not consciously—of the man in the frame.

I think back to what I have known of myself. If there is any continuity, it is only in my memory. Can I let go—*am I letting go*—of the man who only exists in my own picture frames?

Savage Country

One is prompted to ponder, at times, "Who is the most fearsome of animals?"

Well before sundown, I returned from a solitary walk along an unused logging road, a couple of miles into the forest. As I approached within about fifty paces of where I park my camper van—which is approximately one hundred feet from a vacant summer cottage—I heard something crunching branches underfoot among the trees alongside the road. The son of the owner of the cottage sometimes drives out to collect firewood; I looked farther up the road to where he usually parks his pickup truck, and it was not there.

Recognizing that these were not the sounds of the gentle deer, I looked more closely among the trees. Surprised by my proximity—a rustling, mid-June breeze had masked my footfalls—a bear stared at me. This was not a cub, but a mature bear, dark, with a silvery face, and it was close enough that my first reaction was to glance at the terrain behind me.

The bear saw no cause for violence. Still on all fours, it turned and bounded away into the woods.

Days later, at about the same time on a similar day, I walked about a quarter of a mile, in the other direction on the road, to a neighboring cottage. Through the owner of that cottage, I had previously been told that it was being visited by a fundamentalist minister who had recently transferred from the Chicago area to California, and it was suggested that he and his wife might welcome my visit.

Inside the gate, a blond boy, about twelve years old, was playing near a car which had an aerial in the middle of its roof, as police cars do. "Are your folks home?," I asked. He nodded shyly, and watched quizzically as I approached the door and sounded the chime. Inside, a slender man moved quickly out of view, and I heard what—from my experience—is the distinct cocking of a gun. Almost as if by signal, someone in the bedroom, alongside the porch, began dialing a telephone.

Twice I called out, "Hello, there!"

No reply.

I turned and walked back toward my forest.

The Empty Page

Take a piece of paper and draw two horizontal lines on it from edge to edge, with a vertical gap between them. In our "mind's eye", this is typically our conception of time, a ribbon running continuously and evenly from one point to another.

Were I to say, make a mark where we are now—in the "present"—you would likely intersect the two lines somewhere toward the middle. Directed to add "past" and "future", you would probably write the first word about midway to the left of the "present" intersection, and the latter word toward the righthand side.

This is our usual, linear image of time. Now, if we were to discuss the concepts of "past" and "future", and you were to agree with me that in reality only the present truly exists, we could erase those two words.

And, considering that the present is all that there is, we could even erase the intersection which represented the present.

What, now, if we were to come to the realization that time is really without limit, without borders? You are ahead of me: you have already erased the two lines.

The picture we have of time as a continuum is not unconnected to our image of the self as an entity which has continuity in "time", a self which operates within the limitations of "its past" and "its future".

When it is clear to you that the past and the future are a fiction of an ego which seeks endurance, it will be clear to you that the self can be nothing more than an aware presence in any given instant: and so it possesses no particular, fixed construct from moment to moment. You are, in reality, only what you are in any particular instant (and even that which we determined that you "are" is a definitional matter): that is all that you are, ever have been or will be. The moment is constantly changing, you are in the moment, and so there can be no fixed, static entity that you can lastingly identify with.

When your perception of self/time is such as this, your perception of the temporal world is different, effortlessly.

A Wayfarer's Reverie

This fountain is intriguing for its simplicity. It's at a corner of the block that comprises Luther Burbank Home and Gardens, in Santa Rosa. The circular concrete pool is edged with brick steps; in diameter, it could probably be leaped by a healthy horse.

In the center of the pond, protruding just above normal water level, is a single, small water pipe. It shoots a jet of water steadily straight up, a height of probably eight to ten feet. But as the water reaches its equilibrium of gravity, it falls back down around the stem of the pipe. Its splashing impact forces the pond to rhythmically rise and fall; as the water level rises above the mouth of the pipe, it causes the arising column to dissipate somewhat. Thus the water that is falling back from atop meets this weak upward spray, and there's a clash as they both proceed in their natural direction.

No matter where you look at the water on this column that is forced up, something interesting is happening. This is a clear, sunny afternoon—a weekday, with most people at work—and in the sunlight is this pulsating, spurting silvery-white ejaculation. The Yang is thrusting rhythmically straight up, and the Yin pulsing back down around the base of each stroke. The throbbing sound of the splashing water, against the background hum of traffic at Santa Rosa and Sonoma Avenues, is engaging.

There is a point toward the top, where most of the spurt has lost its momentum, that a swift sword could often cut through undampened. But above is a frenzied blob of water—now translucent against the blue sky—springing in ecstasy like a boneless frog as if to explode into a union of essence with the atmosphere. Each gush seems more certain than the one before it to break that barrier that holds it earthbound and to push off like a bubble of mercury into the sky. One after another reach the barrier, regain composure, and come back to their nature.

My first instinct is one of possession. It occurs to me that this contrivance could become an item of ownership; that a facsimile could be constructed in a yard somewhere for the personal enjoyment of the fountain's display. I want somehow to take this amusement somewhere, to freeze it into some place where it will conveniently be mine, like a butterfly in a glass paperweight.

Can I sit here for half an hour, perhaps an hour, and simply enjoy this sight, this sound, this soft mist that blows to me from the spray and disappears?

Self as Time

Draw, with your finger, a square, in the air in front of you; then draw a connecting line, from one side of the square to the other side. This transference of your finger—from Point A on one side of the perimeter, to Point B on the other side—represents what we know as "time": we would say that it took "one-tenth of a second" for the object to travel from Point A to Point B. Time is, essentially, a measurement in space.

We tend to think of space as the empty atmosphere that stretches out all around us. But such arbitrary locations as "Point A" or "Point B" are the designates within which space is contained, or confined, whether technically we are referring to empty air or solid matter: "The bullet entered at Point A, and exited at Point B, penetrating the entire space of the four inches of wood." When a space is defined, it is normally defined as a measurement of some particular distance, however general: "for as far as the eye can see" is a typical referent to the dimensions of our casual concept of space.

To the best of man's knowledge—empirically, through the instruments of science, and intuitively, through sensory observation—the reality of ultimate space is that, somehow, it is without end, without definable borders. It is a space in which there are no fixed coordinates, except those which are chosen for designation or appointment. On an objective basis, the relationship between any perceivable subjects in space is entirely relative.

Time, then, as an eventual measurement of necessarily-relative phenomena in space, must itself be relative. Space being endless, and time being a measurement of space, universal time is endless; without a perceivable beginning or ending, all calculations involved in it are calculations between arbitrarily-chosen events among all of the possible, relative events.

Time, more accurately, is a measurement of (or, since coordinates are needed, between) movements in space. We would say that there is, principally, space; there is the relative movement of "objects" in space; and there is the measurement of activity or movement, which we call time.

You, as the finger, appear in space; you move from Point A (your beginning) to Point B (your ending), and this progression is calibrated in time. But where birth began and where death ends is entirely relative. Thus the existence of the individual self is likewise indefinite—a matter of definition.

Worldly Citizenship

The squirrels and pigeons seem to be tolerant of each other. They are on the ocean side of the fence that runs as a barrier along the bluff in this Santa Monica park. It is a Sunday afternoon, still sunny before the fog is to roll in. A trim, middle-aged man in a faded blue cap is tossing birdseed over the fence rail, with a pound or so still left in the cloth bag. About a dozen iridescent, slate gray pigeons are waddling and crouching through the birdseed, a wavy sea of bobbing heads. From a hole under the sidewalk, a healthy, spotted squirrel watches, then creeps out with belly flat along the earth, entering the sea of pigeons from their edge. Soon another squirrel follows, and both move along among the pigeons, vacuuming up the birdseed. The man scatters more birdseed, so that there's room for everyone.

A heavyset woman, carrying a paper bag, walks up to his elbow. "God bless you!" She smiles at him and, dipping into the paper bag, tosses the flock their next handful of birdseed. She is followed by a large man in sunglasses, who appears to be Jewish.

"We feed them all the time," the woman continues. She has a European accent.

"What country are you from?" the smaller man asks. He too has an accent.

"Hun-gary."

"Christian?"

"Yes."

"I'm Muslim."

The woman's companion joins the conversation. "What do you pay for your birdseed? We get ours for $3.80, and we always get at least the five-pound size."

"I get the same."

"What place are you from?"

"Istanbul."

The man exclaims to his companion, "Hey, I'll bet he could tell you about that place you want to go to!"

"You want this?" The man from Istanbul offers to pour his remaining birdseed from his cloth bag into the paper bag. She accepts.

"First we want to go to Israel," she tells him. Then she describes a tour of cities and islands that would follow. She names a particular place and asks him what he knows about the people there.

The man folds his cloth bag and puts it in his jacket pocket.

"They don't like Jews!," he says, and walks away.

The squirrels and pigeons are milling about, on their side of the fence, looking for any birdseed they may have missed among them.

As long as man is competitive, war serves a purpose; it is the ultimate testing ground.

Even less aggressive cultures than ours—such as the American Indians—found a justification for warring, as a field in which one might display courage. It has been observed that pride is perhaps the deadliest of all of mankind's sins. Pride is the half-brother of greed. And greed is the least acknowledged justification for war.

While greed is our least admitted motivation, pride is socially acceptable. Conditioned to pride, as we are, it is most subtly woven into the fabrication which we esteem as the self. The image of the self is a stimulus for pride, and pride is a stimulus for the self...achievement being the ideal reaction.

Comparison, and resultant envy, is at the root of pride, and, combined with fear, also at the root of greed. It is pride, envy, fear and greed which cause us to stand apart in isolation from others, rather than to cooperate in our mutual interest. Even in cooperation, man finds it difficult to resist the attraction of achievement, and its consequent pride, as his goal. Cooperation does not necessarily lead to an ending of aggression; we must first understand what it means to compare, and also to desire the socially-acceptable gratification of control.

Seeking Change

If there is something—such as primal energy—which is in existence in every possible place, that is the equivalent of saying, from a different perspective, that it exists nowhere in particular. Thus it is sometimes said, in mystical writings, that that which is to be found nowhere is, ironically, everywhere. "Those who cannot see It everywhere will find It nowhere."

Such is the essence of time. Time does not exist, except by man's definition. It is a measure of the observation of change, from one arbitrary point or stage to another. Thus even that phenomenon which we call "change" is definitional and dependent upon an analytical brain to measure and compare such abstract absolutes as "change" or "no change". But intuitively we sense that there is a primal energy which is in existence everywhere, and that this primal energy manifests as the pulsations of change. Thus change is universal, and, by extrapolation, time is universal.

When we observe within the context of that which exists everywhere, we recognize that there is no designated locus such as "up" or "down", no inside or outside, no right nor left. Within the framework of that which is everywhere, there is no justification or need for the type of linear, measurable movement which is so comfortable for the mind of man. Thus, in the realm of universal change, change does not seek a direction that is intended to satisfy the logic of the brain that is perceiving it.

In other words, in *change*—or primal energy—there are no such compartments as "past", "present" or "future", nor are there convenient alignments of phenomenon which follow a perpendicular trajectory. Change is at each and every point in every trajectory, acting in every possible direction in any instant.

Primal energy, being everywhere at every conceivable time, is at once the cause of everything and the result of everything. To the cosmos, one could say, cause and effect are not separate, they are the same thing. Indeed, there is but one constant in the universe, and it is change—the manifestation of primal energy. Put another way, in all the world of things which are conceivable in the mind of man, there is but one thing: that which is at every point of matter/energy, in every instant or space of time.

Primal energy is at the essence of every moment and of everything which exists in any moment. Within you and this moment are all that there is. What more could be sought?

One Day, at a Time

(Finishing his thermos of coffee and replacing it in the tote bag, he takes up a notebook for a "pencil sketch.")

The campground is behind me. I have come along a rarely-used dirt trail to its end, along a dry creek bed, and have taken a clear spot in the shade of an oak tree. An old folding chair has been left here from my previous visits, and I am fully bare in it, this grand and gorgeous day, with my tanned feet on the soil.

It is a couple of hours before noon, mid-April, and the air temperature is perhaps 70° where I sit. The breeze will usually keep pace with the heat in this canyon, throughout the day, and so now it just stirs the reddish foxtail grass before me and waves the fingers of the silvery-green wild oats on both sides of the trail. At the ranch, out of sight on the other side of the creek though on higher ground, I can hear their prideful display of patriotism—a flag—snapping with each gust. From the nearby road I sometimes hear a passing truck or motorcycle, and sometimes I hear the bark of the ranch dog or distant voices from the RV campground, and of course there are occasional private planes headed toward the airport near El Cajon. Otherwise the sounds are those of nature: the breezy stirring of the leaves, the birds, the insects.

The sky is without a blemish, it is barely blue and if one focuses on any particular point it almost appears white or gray. It is the backdrop for a gentle hill which looms directly before me and causes the trail's end. Somehow the breeze all but neglects this hill; it usually seems still, as if cut from a pastoral oil painting and pasted on the pale blue matboard. There are stippled suggestions of charcoal shade beneath its flat green shrubs amidst splotches of golden-rod yellow.

In the foreground, clearly visible to me, is the pale yellow of wild mustard which sways on the slope on either side of the trail. Placed in the garden—as nature gardens—between it and the wild oats are orange-and-yellow open shrubs of the pea family. And raising themselves among the shrubbery, in one spot, are the white bells of the morning glory. And of course there is the sprawling tendrils of the wild cucumber; the dandelion; the recumbent glossy foliage of the poison oak.

(He pauses to eat a fig newton and scan the hill.)

It is surprising how little wildlife one sees, as one sits here for hours quietly in this quiet spot, and yet there remains a variety of wildlife. There is an occasional tiny brown ant which starts on a toe and explores harmlessly the body and the lawn chair; a caterpillar intrigued with the tote bag; a butterfly at rest on a sandal or atop my straw hat; a bumblebee—for whom flight is impossible, according to man's theoretical understanding of the principles of aerodynamics—who is flitting from flower to field, humming as she works; there are the little black flies and the gnats which—if not discouraged—hover right in front of your eyes.

Keeping their distance are the little lizards gliding noisily through the dry oak leaves near your chair; there is an occasional squirrel to be seen near the more distant oak trees; and, one day, two roadrunners crossed the trail and ran up the embankment, one after another. But one can watch for hours without a sight of a coyote, though nearby is a patch of matted grass where they apparently lay at night.

(Drops pencil to swat a pesky fly—unsuccessfully.)

There is a wren diligently inspecting the lower shrubs; a sparrow perched close enough to curiously observe the writer; a hummingbird whose brief survey turns up no red flowers here; a jay who forsakes a desultory prospecting, among the fallen oak leaves, for the easier pickings at the campground.

And, more distant above the hill, are the black silhouettes of the soaring buzzards, the gregarious and vocal ravens, and the lone red-tailed hawk.

I have overdone my exercises recently (again!) and my back is sore, and so I have skipped today's exercises and swim in the pool in favor of a longer sit, by an hour or so, in this quiet spot, on this scrumptious day. I will likely walk for awhile, before fixing my dinner, and may sit in stillness again before bedtime, probably in the darkened campground "clubhouse", whose glass patio doors provide a softly-lit night view of the park-like grounds. Soon, it may be warm enough at night to sit outside, under the clearly starry sky, and I would welcome that.

What does it mean to live in the moment, to live day by day, to take no thought for the night to come, let alone for the morrow?

The I-deal

One comprehends the idealism in attempting to maintain a life of consistent comfort and gratification. And so, in reaction, one resolves to abandon such a pursuit entirely and to instead give oneself up to the life of a bird, to emulate the life of a penniless, homeless Jesus who had not where to lay his head. Are not both endeavors pursuing an ideal?

Any depiction of a situation in the future is an idea, and an idea is always the basis of the ideal.

Our first and foremost ideal is that we ought not to lose our physical life, to die, within any period of time which we can distinctly imagine. Our second ideal is that we ought to be happy for as long as we shall live. Our third ideal is that, in the absence of happiness, we ought at least to be free of suffering, pain.

The central issue of your *life* is your *death*. Living is—*is*—dying. To imagine any personal moment of life beyond the present moment is merely an idea; it is to aspire to an ideal situation. Tomorrow, we are any of us—in this fact of life—as dead as alive. That may be ideal to one who is in agony, perceiving freedom from pain to be ideal; in the absence of ideas, it is merely 'what is.'

The central idea underlying ideals is that of cause and effect: through choice and control we can direct the impersonal energy, which we call change, toward our personal, objectified ideal.

In expecting change to respond to the bidding of our individual will, we divert our attention from the only present moment which there is, to a future moment which there isn't. To expect is to await; to await is to focus one's attention on a future moment which does not exist. To expect happiness, to await happiness, is not to be happy. The *pursuit* of happiness is not happiness; it is pursuit. 1 is a number, 1.0 is a number with expectations. Our expectation is, first, that there is a future moment for us which will arrive, and, second, that we can personally shape the content of that moment.

Our primary ideal is that some particular situation will become "better" (or, at least, not "worsen"), will improve. To identify the "better" or the "worse" is to compare. Comparison, coupled with desire, leads to choice—the choice of the more ideal situation or outcome. Choice is the first factor in the attempt to control. Control begets resistance. Resistance galvanizes, polarizes; it is the fulcrum between the dualities. The wider the dualities, the more compelling is the comparison and the more imperative the choice. The noose of idealism constricts.

To die to choice is to die to desire (such as the desire for relief from anguish, pain), to die to the choice of the ideal. The death of choice is death without choice.

Desire may wear the face of wishing things to be different than they are, or wear the face of wanting things to remain the same. Wherever there is an ideal, there is desire seeking something other than 'what is.' Control, and resistance, are never far behind.

The 'what is' is not ideal; it is reality, not an idea. There is not balance in the universe, there is dynamic imbalance. Primal energy manifests, but does not control. The basic "control" of the universe is that there is no single thing in control. Separation implies exclusion. The control which sunlight has over dew is to absorb it in its attention.

The embodiment of action is stillness. Ask for what you need by being so still that you await nothing. Even death need not be awaited; as with all things, it is in this present moment—the moment of the 'what is,' which we never find ideal.

News from the Ravine

Several feet ahead and to the side of me, in full sun on the slope, a shrub has caught my eye. From its base, several long spires of stalk rise several feet, almost straight toward the sky, and are notched every half foot or so with small leaves.

Growing in among the leafy base of the plant is a sprawling white morning glory. One long tendril of this interloper has wound itself up along the shortest of the host plant's ascendant stalks. Within the last few inches of this stalk, the morning glory has sent out a single, slender tendril, with a few leaves along its stem all the way to its tip.

From its departure point, this tendril grows nearly horizontal and unsupported for what appears to be about a foot and a half. It is slightly kinked in a couple of places, much like a snake would be, indeed has a rigidity similar to the muscular snake, and it even slightly raises itself toward its tip suggestive of the head of a snake.

What interests me is that if we were to look down on the host stalk from above and view it as a central point from which radiate degrees of circumference, there would be 360 directions in which this morning glory tendril might choose to point. And it is, of course, pointing in one of these directions.

Approximately two feet to the side of the host stalk is the next-nearest stalk of the shrub, this one another foot or more higher than the host stalk. The morning glory tendril is pointing directly at this next most-promising position.

At the time I first observe this, the potential stalk is at least a couple of inches out of reach of the tendril's tip. As I write this about an hour later, without in any way having changed my viewing position, the tendril now touches the stalk.

There is a gentle breeze blowing. Usually it moves the potential stalk and the host stalk in the same direction, but the host stalk is shorter and has the ballast of the morning glory tendril wound around it, and so sometimes the taller stalk is blown toward it. The tendril, being lightest of all, also sometimes wafts upward with the breeze, like a snake about to strike.

But I can see, when the breeze is not blowing, that it is not such random mechanics which has brought the tendril closer to its target.

The tendril could, with one sudden straightening of its kinks, make a lunge toward the leafy notches of the target stalk, and possibly it would lodge there. But if it failed, it seems that it would have lost the tension which keeps it erect. It, instead, is patiently persistent. It is not in a hurry to go anywhere.

Without artifice, it has somehow grown—in my short watch of a couple of hours—closer to its target, and now touches, for moments between breezes, the objective support. The tip is now slightly curled, like a shepherd's crook; one opportune breeze will now likely do the rest.

I must soon end my visit, but I have no doubt that when I return tomorrow, the tendril will be winding its way toward the tip of this second host stalk.

I suppose one could have watched this—in a few minutes—on a nature program on television, thanks to stop-motion photography. This wonder would have been sandwiched between countless inane commercials, and would have appeared no more miraculous than Jiminy Cricket popping out from between two Oreo cookies.

But the plant and I have spent an intimate afternoon together, and neither one of us was in any hurry from the start.

Is it possible to be free and at the same time to be dependent? Is freedom an abstraction or is it integral to a vital life?

We humans are—as are all things—interdependent. Dependence implies support and therefore attachment. To that which you are tethered, your freedom is contingent, limited.

To "become" independent, as a reaction to dependence, is an activity in time, a "gaining" idea; the image of the self which was dependent is now involving independence in defining the image of the self. Upon what, actually, is the image of the self dependent, interdependent or independent?

Where is freedom to be found, for the human animal, until there is freedom from image and the coercive ideal? That which is truly free is boundless; where are the bonds of the self which has never existed from the start? Upon what, but imagination, can any abstraction be dependent?

Vacating the Mind

Let us say that you are a brain cell. Among your biological functions, you are a repository for the bytes of information commonly referred to as memory. It is your task to absorb and retain the significant data which is transmitted to you, without questioning or examining the value of the content. Therefore, you receive impartially that which, for their special uses, either the "autonomic" (precognitive) or the "speculative" (thinking) aspects of the mind, or consciousness, submit to you.

For example: today, for the first time in your recollection, one of the fingers has come into contact with something known as Stinging Nettle; you have been called upon, by that portion of the mind which regulates instinctual responses, to store a visual "snapshot" of a nettle leaf for possible future recall.

Shortly after, the thinking mind involved its self in the composition of a limerick concerning an Old Maid of Sheboygan, and it has been your lot to absorb every stanza.

You are saturated with such material, accumulated over many years, and virtually as much miscellany as you are required to store, you are also required to retrieve and divulge—at any given moment. And this is only *one* of the myriad, diverse activities which is your responsibility—every instant of the day or night.

Tonight has been the most unusual night of your experience. The body has sat down in a comfortable chair, after a light supper. There is one small, dim light in the room. There is quiet, except for some faint sounds of remote activity or movement. You are busy, as usual, responding to the needs of the autonomous mind; aiding the hands, without the assistance of conscious thought, to adjust a pillow behind the back; assisting the eyes in their movement and focus, and so on. You are bracing yourself, meanwhile, for the typical barrage of "inactive" activity generated by the reasoning portion of the mind: evocation of images filed under "Past"; replay of audio-imaginative laugh-tracks, from "Emotions: Positive"; a re-review of previously reviewed views and postponed provocative postulates, etc.

But while you are focused on hovering alertly over the keyboard, the pattern is not being followed tonight. The eyes have rested on a softly-lit teacup, and have not been motivated to move from there. The ears are listening to the muted, outdoor sounds as one would listen to a chirping sparrow—

without attempting to identify the theme, without analysis or comparison or judgement, without conscious effort in recognizing the source.

Indeed, this body tonight appears to be that of a child, sitting alone in its room with no compulsion to do anything in particular or to be anyone, or anywhere, special…not even consciously "relaxing" or engaged in "quieting the mind." The evocative mind is quieting itself, without insistence or control. It has been, effortlessly, freed for this moment that is without time.

You, and the other brain cells, are speechless. That busy body, the self, has vacated or died tonight; the hyperactive mind is neither occupied nor pre-occupied. There is no recognized or recognizable or recognizing entity, no identifiable "being" at the helm of consciousness; the raft is drifting aimlessly on the current, and one cannot discern that it is manned or unmanned.

You brain cells are freed from your accustomed activity. You need not, enervatingly, divide your awareness between the trifling excesses of the calculating mind and the continual exigencies of the functional, noncognitive mind. Blissfully, you loose your liberated energy in an awed expression of simple serenity.

Sunday Matinee

It is not just quiet today, it is still. It is a stillness which you can almost hear, or feel. It is not a stillness in which the grasses are not rehearsing their Ballet to the Breeze, but there is a silence of the earth.

Past noon, it is likely the warmest day we've had this year. You can hear the birds, but you scarcely note any movement. Even the flies and bees are all but absent. It is a day in which a limb can suddenly drop from a tree.

And, there is quiet. Mother's Day: perhaps everyone in this hemisphere is at dinner with their mother. Even the few airplanes seem remote, and the atmosphere is clear without the slightest haze. It's breathtaking.

The colors are rich. The pale blue sky, the dark green of the tight oak leaves against their shadowy branches; the wild garden, up the slope, with dark blue spikes that appear, from here, to be larkspur, and the pink of what looks like godetia, among the bright yellow of mustard and the glowing white of morning glory; the wild grasses which in the past weeks have yellowed to golden straw; the tan sandy path at the base of your bare feet.

Few can afford the luxury of this time and place: a Sunday afternoon in spring in a wooded ravine. To be here now is too expensive: it is to give up a day of golf; to forego the washing of the car; to ignore obligations; to forsake companionship—all prices to be paid for being civilized.

Civilization and stillness—quiet, inactivity—do not go together. Civilization is a continual process of choices; stillness comes without choice. There is nothing which can be done to create this stillness. It is not something which is to be acquired; it has no value as currency. It is, put another way, priceless.

One must relax, to breathe this stillness. Not just the body: the mind, the psyche. One must relax ambition. Ambition and stillness are not compatible. There is no ticking of the clock here. There is no effort in stillness.

While our jaded mind welcomes variety, the mind of man, in general, fears change. Though we are aware that change is constant, the changes in nature are unpredictable. And so it is not change per se that we fear, but its unpredictability.

We select our friends, and elect political leaders, on the basis of their predictability. To be unpredictable is equated with being dangerous, and these are sometimes synonymous in the description of wild animals.

To be predictable is to follow a pattern; it is a retracing of the past onto the present and upon the future. Who is free of convention and conformity can least be depended upon to be predictable. And we are attached to the comfort of dependence.

To break our patterns is to threaten our sense of security; patterns predict an outcome, and our eye is usually fastened on a goal. To be free in this moment is to be free of our patterns of the past, and our expectations for the future. That which is unbounded is poised in any direction.

Where there is a plan, there is effort. Where there is effort, there is attachment to result. Where there is attachment, there is dependence, and dependence is not freedom.

A plan is bondage to the dual polarities that we call cause and effect. Effect is dependent upon cause, and a subsequent cause is dependent upon effect. That which is circuitously bound is the subject of manipulation, interference. Interference is the conflicting antithesis of a plan. Any plan bears the seeds of its own conflict.

We can choose for the "better", we can choose for the "worse", or we can neglect choice and relinquish our attachment to the outcome. Choices are relative to future eventualities. Where the future is unknown—as it must be, in order to be the future—choice is irrelevant.

Plans for the self's future are necessary only to the sustenance of the self. The self which must be sustained by its own volition is a self caught under the wheel of cause/effect. The self defines its plan, and the planning defines the self.

No Reason

Had I not abandoned reason, I would be in conflict. I have no reason to write, and yet I do it. There is nothing more satisfying than to sit here for hours, attentive to the beauty in the day wrapped around me. I have no motivation to take my eyes from the satin blue sky, the scrubby green hills, the sunlight and shadows of the oak tree, and to focus them instead on a lined-paper pad—and yet something motivates me. The writing appears without any real effort on my part, but I am relieved when I can again turn away from it.

Sitting here in the daytime is a treat for the eyes, for they can freely and eagerly roam from the circling buzzard above the horizon to the sunbathing lizard near my feet. But the mind knows that this is also the time when writing can take place.

After dark, I often take a glass of hot green tea and a couple of oatmeal cookies, and I sit for a few hours when the clubhouse is deserted. With the lights out, I open the sliding glass door and pull a chair up to face the darkened campground. There is little occasion for the eye to roam within this dimmed framework, and so the motionless sitter might appear to others to be in a trance-like condition. Under the circumstances, the mind would not consider this an occasion for writing, though I do sometimes jot a note or two on a notepad from the pocket of my robe.

Writing is unimportant, and the sitting—the meditation or contemplation—is in no way a vehicle for the writing. Meditation is not properly a vehicle for anything, for it is not a means to an end; it is end *and* means. One sits quietly in the realization that there is nothing of more immediate importance that one can do.

To know thyself is to know that there is no self to know. The self is merely another aspect of unending change. There can be no self which is not in the moment, and all that is of the moment is change. We can never know change as a static thing, but only learn from it as an expression of our truly unidentifiable self. We are, individually or collectively, the teacher, the teaching and the taught.

The thoughtful mind avoids stillness, for that is the residence of the empty self. When thought carries itself to its natural conclusion, it is at the threshold of the empty mind—the mind without ideas, even of its self. Stillness is the expression of emptiness, which is the death of the self.

The Open Mind

I sit here inside this room, which has four walls, a ceiling and a floor. It appears, superficially, that I am within a container. But when I acknowledge that all things in the universe are but an energy in its myriad forms—including the walls of this room—the "container," as a form, falls away from me.

When I further acknowledge that I, too, am nothing but this energy, there is not even anything that is to be contained within a container. Put another way, I and the container are the same.

Most of us envision that our mind is a container—perhaps not with six sides, like a cube, and perhaps not even spherical; but we generally tend to suppose that our mind is contained within a particular periphery…such as our body, or our brain.

Sitting here in this room, one would likely presume that his mind is at least within the confines of the room, and not sprawling somewhere outside of the walls, But if one were sitting somewhere out on the desert—with only the sky above, from horizon to horizon—what then might one presume to be the container, the spatial borders of one's mind?

Each and every cell has an intelligence which we would call consciousness; it is, as it were, conscious of the situation immediately around it. Therefore, the body—*your body*—is imbued with consciousness.

But this is not a separate, individuated consciousness; it is the same consciousness, or intelligence, common to every cell everywhere, to every molecule, to all of matter and its elementary energy.

There is a brain which is unique to each of our unique bodies, or forms; and this brain is composed of cells, molecules, which embody consciousness. While this brain, with its ability to postulate, might conclude that this consciousness is a property which exists within its own exclusive limits, in so doing it establishes an imaginary boundary. Our thoughtful image is that our bodies tend a consciousness which is ancillary to our brain, and we refer to this as a "mind." We conclude that our mind, associated with our brain, resides in our head. Consciousness then, by this reasoning, is an allotment which fills each individual skull, and anything which exists outside of the head is not consciousness, is not our mind.

⦁

Man's behavior is motivated by the idea of separation. Where there is division, there is conflict; and where there is division, there is fear and the consequent struggle for dominance and security. Where there is the notion of security, there is resistance to change. Change, the basic element of life, becomes parsed into "good" change and "bad" change. The effort to control change is man's yoke. Choice is division's first step.

⦁

The mind which is common to man does not exist without division. The operative division which the mind makes is that of "self" versus non-self, or "other". In perpetuating the mind's image and acting on behalf of the self, man exhibits such human characteristics as pride, envy, greed, ambition. These traits or characteristics are not uniquely individual but are common to the species which is concerned with the security and sustenance of the self.

We are all of us subject to these traits, to the extent that we regard our self as an entity: in all image, for example, there is comparison and pride, and in all comparison and pride there is image.

When we acknowledge that we are subject to our self image, we face the fact that in each of us there is—to whatever degree—common human reactions such as envy and greed. We can attempt to suppress these symptoms of self-image—to try, for instance, to not be envious—or we can take our attention to the root of our malady: our sense of isolation as a self-ish entity. When the self is clearly seen, it is seen to be without support; in seeing this, it falls away.

Unexpected

It is, somehow, an atypical day. Not just in that a pair of woodpeckers are hammering on a dead branch in the nearby oak tree. And not just in the appearance of the forager among the weeds, a wasp-like insect of about two inches in length, with an iridescent blue-green body and improbable red wings.

Out of the blue sky, above the hill facing my chair, small puffs of cloud will occasionally appear. Unlike down here, where a brisker breeze than usual sometimes shakes out the oak tree's leaves, there appears to be no air movement. And so the fluffy white manifestations ripen to a roundish fullness, and then, in the same tempo, entirely disappear...similar to the appearance of fireworks in the night sky. And, indeed, a faint slip of the moon can be seen off to the side, when nothing else is high-lighting the blue.

To be able to sit without expectation is to be able to live without expectation. Expectation is a shadow which precedes. We desire happiness, we seek it, we await it. We measure its presence, aware always that while happiness is subjective, change is objective; change has no investment in the perpetuation of the perfect cloud.

We do not expect the blue sky to magically produce benign white clouds, nor do we expect the clouds to linger for our delectation. They come, unanticipated, and they go, unlamented.

To be able to sit untroubled by desire is to be able to live untroubled by desire.

・

Naturally, you identify yourself as your self—but you are not your identity. You are really that which you were before there was a self to identify. The mind of thought will not admit to this, because the mind of thought is the mind of the self. To concede that there is no self, consciously, is the end of the self and its particular consciousness.

The nature of the self is self-perpetuation. Because of your reluctance to let go of the self, you will not let got of the triumphs and the failures of the self:

experiences, catalogued in memory, are what define the self. Because you will not let go of your attachment to "your" past and its future, you are the scarred linchpin in the push and pull of your individuated life.

You will not be reasoned into releasing your attachment to your sense of self, because you were conditioned—not reasoned—to your acceptance of it.

·

To attempt to uncondition yourself to your sense of self is to act as subject to object, in a timeframe which stretches—cause/effect—into the future.

Since there is no self which is truly separate from who you really are, there can be no activity (rather, reaction) which reunites the two—in any amount of time.

The death of the self is a perception, which takes place in an instant. It is not dependent upon effort, least of all the effort of logical thought.

Therefore, no one can bring you to this point by reason. Indeed, there is no point to which to be brought, since you are there already—if you but realized it. *Realize* means "to make real." How does one live when one realizes one's true identity?

Uncontrolled

Oddly, it is a quiet and still day, even though it is a holiday. I can hear voices faintly from the tennis and volleyball courts from where I sit, and the campground is as full of visitors and their motorhomes as it has been this year—even though the swimming pool has been drained of water for repairs.

It is a splendidly clear and warm day at the end of May, with a breeze that was not even a challenge for the morning frisbee players. Massage tables were being set up in the shade as I strolled toward the ravine. It's a day for eating watermelon, even if you're not a patriot.

This is the first I've sat here for a couple of days, my weekend schedule interrupted by the flurry of activities. My evening contemplations, for a couple of hours after dark, have also yielded to the clubhouse game nights. I last sat there alone in the darkened room, near the blanketed pool table and bigscreen television and shelves of books, a couple of nights ago. Voices droned across the patio from the crowded jacuzzi, and lights were evident in the community kitchen.

My gaze rested on the dark matting of broad-leafed trees, across the creek—now mossy and nearly dry—which runs through the campground. My thoughts were typically occupying themselves with unimportant matters. I made no effort to still my thoughts. Bereft of energy, they quieted themselves.

Off to one side of my vision, a small movement of light appeared as if reflected from somewhere behind my shoulder and onto the wall. It meandered up the wall and ended in a blob, almost as quickly as I noticed it. My awareness of it was heightened because it was unexplainable.

Immediately, my sense of self was taken out of myself. My eyes were still attending the shadowy trees outside of the open clubhouse door, but the eyes themselves were at the moment unattended. There was, instead, an unusual presence…something other than the presence that I usually associate with myself. It was beyond my control. It arrived unbidden and, briefly, departed unbidden.

The brain attunes itself to what it is free to attune to. When it is free of control, it attunes itself to that which is outside of the realm of control.

Vulnerable

Growing in full sun on the slope ahead of me is a tall, loose, leafy shrub. At the tops of its willowy branches are dainty white doilies of flower. It is cheery, it is open, it is vulnerable. It has settled upon an allotted place in the panoply of living things, and it will fully flower in that place.

From a forager it will not retreat, and it will give of itself what is asked. To a bulldozer it may one day yield its life, and yet will offer no resistance except for its tenacious passivity. To live and to die is 'what is', and—since the two are not separate—there is no time truly to be found between for conjecture.

There was a large bunny alongside the path this morning. It noticed my approach, and paused, motionless. It had no experiential reason to avoid close contact with me, but it was instinctively aware of the danger of proximity to larger animals. Despite this awareness of potential danger to its life, it was fully relaxed and therefore attentive and receptive to its situation. When the moment arrived for it to act in movement, it was not frozen in fear, and it departed with dignity and grace.

On my later return on the path, I saw one of the campground cats dash through a clearing and pounce. It emerged with a large bunny held by the scruff of the neck between its teeth, and, with head held high, the hunter trotted past me—though well out of arm's reach. The helpless bunny appeared to be relaxed, and even dignified. There is grace in life and there is grace in death.

Concern, worry, is the self's way of expressing itself. To plan to control the object of worry is to place the self imaginatively into the future. To attempt to control the object of worry is an act of subjective self-assertion. Anxiety is the normal emotion of the self; simply to contemplate the ending of the image of the self is to heighten this emotion.

We are not free of the effect of anxiety until we are free of the self. And we are not free of the self until we let go of our concern for future developments; the only place in which a self can develop is in the future.

When our attention is on the moment, it is not on the self: the self dies in a timeless moment. The saboteur of attention to the moment is the consciousness of the self…the belief that there is an entity whose fate is to be shaped by the future.

What appears to be troublesome to the self—analytical thoughts about the future—is the self's justification for existence: were there not a self to do the planning, there would not be a self to plan for, and vice-versa. The separate sense of the self is dependent upon the idea that there are fragments, as "past" and "future," of this moment which we call life.

The self which is born, dies. The self which continually dies is continually reborn. A raindrop falls to the earth to reappear again as a drop of water—but not the same drop of water. The self reborn is a changed self…not an "improved" self, but a changed self. It is in these changes that life is reflected, and we effortlessly learn from it. It is these changes which we can observe in the moment of attention.

Perfection is a logical attitude: that which can be made better can be made perfect. Naturally, we find it difficult to conceive of any activity, or inactivity, which relates to the individual, as a procedure that is not bent on "improvement"…because each individual is equated only with its self, and the self maintains continuity in the timely process of "becoming."

The self finds difficulty in logically confronting a development which predicates the ending of the self as an entity, or which does not, at the very least, support the enterprise of self-improvement. It resists any suggestion which does not embody within it a promise of perfection. Since perfection is the product of effort, the self is concerned with the efficacy of expended effort: progress precedes perfection.

There is no perfection, without imperfection. This moment is perfect as it is—filled with imperfection. Infused in this perfect moment is your presence—as imperfect as it is. Your impending perfection will not make this perfect moment more perfect than it is. Where there is no tension between perfection/imperfection, there is no logic for the persistence of comparative self image.

Take No Thought

The most difficult thing for us to perceive is that there is an energy which is in every place at every instant in time. There is no place—never has been and never will be—where it is not. Therefore it is all that there is. It is every manner of form and of emptiness.

It being all things at once, there is no point at which it begins or ends. It is the unending movement which we call life, and it is, simultaneously, the point of stillness which we call death. Its manifestation is change.

It being all things, there is no division. Its myriad forms are as different as the hill and the stream, but they are not divided. Having no boundaries or borders, there is nothing which it is separate from. You are It, as are any of its forms or non-forms.

It being without a center, there is not anything which is centrally in control. Being all things, there is no subject to exert control on any object; being without beginning and end—measureless and timeless—there need be no concern for the uncontrolled outcome.

It being all things, it has no identity, apart from who identifies it. The Identifier and the Non-Identifier are both the Identified. To know your true identity and to not know your true identity are the same to that which is itself Identity.

Who does not recognize his true identity identifies with the subject of thought, the "self." Who recognizes his true identity recognizes that there is, in truth, no identity—or as some would say, but one identity. In a universe in which there is no division, there cannot be "self" and "other", "man" and "God," subject in contraposition to object.

There is but this one timeless moment and all the wonder within it. There is nowhere to go, nothing to do, nothing to be. There is nothing to get. You are It.

Post Meridiem

It is after eight-thirty in the evening, and the sky, cloudless and without haze, has darkened. There is the soft light of half a moon between the oak trees, and you now sit—unlike the daytime—out of the shade. The Dipper stretches the length of the break between the trees, and Polaris is to the front and side of you.

It is still warm enough to be wearing only a tee-shirt and a sarong beneath your robe, and you have brought along a sweatshirt for a later hour. The breeze has become but a presence, a conveyor for the hay-like aroma of the dried grasses.

The insects are stilled, save for the throbbing strum of the crickets. A large bird—an owl, perhaps—glides quietly from tree to tree, silhouetted above the light and dark shadowy forms of vegetation on the outlined hill.

A ranch dog has found something to bark about, and the coyotes in the hills parody this with an offering of howls, yowls, yips and screams. The dog shuts up.

Presently, there is a movement among the dried oak leaves which suggests that a rabbit is cautiously hopping nearer to where you are—perhaps the one which earlier browsed within four feet of your chair.

Then there is quiet peacefulness, this night, and you are of it.

It is interesting that man's characterization of "good" and "bad" both have their representation in human-like images, anthropomorphized as God and Satan. And it is presumed that both will co-exist, in opposition, until the end of time.

If there were any such things as "goodness," it could be viable only in this moment. It must thus be conditional to, or relative to, the express circumstances of the moment. This means that goodness would therefore change from instance to instance. Goodness would be, therefore, a relative condition—not to be absolutely attained.

Since that which is good is in the moment, one cannot prepare for its occurrence—except by being attentive to the moment.

To be attentive to the moment is to be cooperative—not resistant—with the 'what is.' Planning, conformism, the attempt to establish a lasting state of goodness, is a striving for a security which is viewed as missing. To conform is to trade the unfolding of the present for the pattern of the past. Conformity is the acting out of social conditioning and collective belief. It is to be who you think you ought to be, rather than who you are.

Sufficient Unto The Day...

This is a day for those felicitous wooly crops of clouds, which—as if viewing them from above—resemble a herd of sheep. They have now aligned themselves into tidy rows, or waves, and amble across the horizon toward an unseen pasture gate. As they dissipate, they are followed by faint, loose tufts, suggestive of scattered bits of wool blown after the herd.

Against the blue field of sky, a redtailed hawk hangs motionless in the air, weaving slightly to accommodate the atmospheric winds, then gently flaps its wings and banks into a turn. It is flying too high, one judges, for an effective session of hunting; and, indeed—as one watches—it appears that the hawk's attention is devoted to enjoyment of flight, and the search for food has taken secondary priority. For thousands of years, there have been hawks that have abandoned themselves freely and entirely to the substance of the moment, and yet the needs of the species has duly been met. Instinctively, this hawk seems to sense that there is no need for chronic concern for the future for one who is capable of full engagement with the moment.

Nothing is permanently settled in the universe. There being but one reality, there is no fixed reality which bears the banner of Security; the singular mind of man is preoccupied with the ideal. To live fully in *this* moment is to abandon the idea of control in relationship to time.

The driving ambition to be in any situation other than the situation you're presently in is the root of the misery of man; its seed is comparison, germinated in the conceptual medium of time. Ideas of "past" and "future" evaporate in the intensity of attention to the moment. Attention without exclusion is meditation. To be choicelessly attentive is to be still. Stillness is not an idea, nor an ideal.

Morning After

Where I sit—with a brushy hill looming before me like a sand dune, and sloping embankments on both sides of me which block views of neighbors—I contemplate a couple of the untamed acres of the world. There are no roads in view, no habitations, no telephone wires or satellite dishes, no fences, no signs of the hand of man. And I have my back turned to civilization, as it exists at the campground.

The day after a holiday, it is quiet enough for the birds to respond to each other's call at some distance. I could just as well be sitting in any reasonably remote part of the world.

At the tent site, about fifty feet behind me on the path, the car with the weekend campers has left. They picked up their cigarette butts, which had been evident before, and put them in the covered trash can. However, on my way past the picnic table this morning, a swarm of flies and the vagrant breeze drew my attention to where one of the campers had defecated on the ground, about fifteen feet from the picnic table. This was left uncovered, as was whatever toilet paper hadn't been blown or carried away, though there were ample handfuls of loose sand, within three feet away, to cover it.

We are a peculiar species, which has the intellect to visualize and to idealize a world imbued with peace, brotherhood, beauty. Yet we haven't the presence of mind to attend to the simplest acts of momentary consideration for our neighbors. Man's seeming ability to desecrate all that he encounters is most noticeable in the places he least frequents: no quiet spot in the wild is felt to be complete until penetrated by a four-wheel-drive with blaring radio, yapping dog, the sounds of rifle shot, broken beer bottles, watermelon rind, candy wrappers and cigarette butts.

But this ravine is, almost, uninhabited today. And when I too return to the campground, civility, peace and natural beauty will resume in it.

Inseparable

Our speculative words "cause" and "reason" are nearly synonymous. Any definitional "cause" has its roots in the past, its blossoming "effect" in the future; in the present it "becomes". This moment, which has no cause to be, has no ascertainable beginning—or ending; no starting time or place, or finishing time or place. Where does a wave indisputably begin or end? Similarly, the coming and going of a tornado is all one movement. This moment is such a movement, a moment of constancy, in which actions are indiscernible one from another. When all things are here and now, the beginning and ending are here and now; the beginning is not "over there", when the ending is here; and the ending is not "later", when the beginning is now. Since the moment is without beginning or end, and life and death are in the moment, life and death are without beginning/ending…constantly and mutually present.

The fox gives birth to (or sires) a baby fox, which eventually gives birth to (or sires) a baby fox; where is the beginning and where is the ending? The material constituents in sperm transit from one human body to another, where a third human body is formed—in a cycle of endless reproduction of matter. A human body grows from a merging of ovum and sperm; the ovum and sperm have materialized from other substances; this human body eventually decays, and its properties return to elemental substances; these elements will nourish other bodies, and form the constituents for such things as ovum and sperm: a body is a particular transitional point in the cycle of elemental substances, with no starting place or stopping place.

Considering that the body has no beginning and no ending, can the self have an end or beginning? And if it has no beginning or end, can there be such a container as the self?

Our concept of life is not merely beginning/ending, but beginning—time—ending...beginning/"coming to be"/ending. Does fall become winter? Or is fall dying, as winter is birthing? Does the bud become a leaf, or does the bud die, simultaneously, with the birth of the leaf? There is no impartial point where the bud first began or the leaf finally ended. A living leaf drops from the tree; at what point do we pronounce it dead?

Death is constancy, not continuity. It is on the same spiral as life, at the same time. It is not on the other end of the football field, rushing forward to tackle life. They are on a tandem bicycle; destruction is present at every creation, and creation present at every destruction. And one of them does not complete its task, then begin the task of the other—move toward the other's field of operation. Their field of operation is the same field of operation. Were creation never to completely do what creation does, destruction would not be able to do what destruction does.

If death was not absolute, there would be no new beginnings—there would be only continuation of old beginnings. Life is not a transition into death, and death is not a transition back to life, a revolving door of consciousness/unconsciousness ("Now I'm reunited with God...Now I'm reunited with man."). Death is destruction, annihilation of all activity that preceded its activity (however gradual), including the activity of the component which is life; it is the negation, impartial negation, of life. Life does not at some point switch careers, and don the helmet of death. Life and death are facets of the same stone, each with its own pristine refraction.

Creation derives from a Sanskrit word, meaning "to bring out of nothing". That space which measureless silence—devoid of conflict—fills, is the space where the energy of destruction prevails. The energy of creation does not share that space, it coincides there. There is space such as this in the empty mind, and energy such as this in the activities of love. The mind that is constantly dying is constantly creating.

Neither creation nor destruction depend on subjective consciousness for inception or expression. Put the perimeter of thought around creation, and what lies outside is the contrasting and isolated antithesis, destruction. Remove the grid of fear and control, and there is only the movement of energy active in freedom.

Neither creation nor destruction, life or death, are "re-doing" anything, nor are they resisting or assisting 'what is'; they *are* what is. In life or death, one is inseparable, undifferentiated, from what is. There is no returning to, or reuniting with, this source which one has never left and can in no way escape or evade.

Bring On The Clowns

The lizards have begun to expect me here. They—or perhaps one in particular—seem to take delight in passing between my feet.

About ten feet ahead of where I usually place my chair, there is a hole to one side of the path, about the size of a dime, which one of them sometimes disappears into. Today's actor has made several attempts to enter, but gets no further in than its hind legs before it pops out again, as if something or someone were blocking or forbidding entry. It then sometimes scampers off among the dried grass and leaves.

Or, it comes to a shadier spot within a dozen or so inches of my foot, and sprawls on its tummy there, looking coyly up at me like a puppy. It resembles a chameleon, is dark brown like the sand here (it's posing for me now, full length), has a head and striping like a garter snake, with a reddish throat. It's possibly ten inches long—about half of that is tail—and as big around as a fountain pen. I can see the wrinkles where its body curves; I can see it blink, and respirate. The little brown ants and the bigger red ants crawl over or along the lizard as if it were a stick on the path. To one side of the lizard, a hover fly appears to be laying eggs in the sand.

The lizard darts off and demonstrates its flexibility, as if to add that to my description. It enters a larger hole—perhaps an abandoned snake hole, about the size of a quarter—head first. I see the tip of the tail sticking out; the tail disappears, and, as quickly, the lizard emerges head first. It has made a complete turnaround in what is possibly a very narrow entryway.

Two jays seem to be disputing territory with a dove, in the oak tree which shades me. The shadow of one of the birds flashes on the ground, near the lizard, simultaneous with a squawk. The lizard scurries up the embankment.

Coexistence is an idea of man. There being but one energy, there is only existence and non-existence.

We can designate as "physical" time the time of the arrow in flight, "psychological" time as the continuation of a past into a present and thence into a future.

A seed occupies an actual, physical space; a personality does not. A seed "grows" in physical time; a personality "improves" in psychological time. The expectation of childbirth is a matter of physical time; the expectation of "personal growth" is in psychological time.

Since you cannot put your finger on the locality of a personality, it cannot move, in actuality, from place to place (except within the spaciousness of the imagination). An apple seed becomes an apple tree; a "person" does not become a "better" (or "worse") person, except by definition.

There is *only* change, and not anything apart which is changing.

·

The presence of knowledge in the mind, is dependent upon time, in the mind. Insight is not dependent upon any time except that which exists outside of the mind—this present, eternal moment. It is presented to those who are awake in the moment, who are not focused on the dead past or the unborn future.

Insight leaps the gap which linear thought can only attempt to bridge. It is free to appear when the horizon-to-horizon cloud cover of thought has opened to a clearing. And typically, it suggests unconventional action or behavior.

The perception that it is the climate of stillness which permits clarity is insight. This perception is not thought, but action. Seeing is an action, and the stillness to see is of that action.

Desire is the mainspring of the self, and choice is the expression of desire. Choice is animated by the ambition to control. We attempt to control that to which we are attached, and in so doing find ourselves to be the subject of the object of our desires.

In control, there is embedded resistance. We contradictorily attempt, throughout our day, to assist and to resist the energy of change. Who is choiceless is free of attachments and ambition on their behalf, free of resistance to change, and free of being controlled by choice and its subsequent resistance. Who is free of choice meets death without desire, without resistance.

Time is Comparison

The grasses on the slope, on both sides of the path, are still pleasing to behold, but they are different than they were one month ago. Now they are dry straws, more brittle in the breeze.

Coming here today, and comparing their flat hue to the lustrous green of last month, we would say that they are dead. But on what day would we declare that they had died?

Change, though as subtle, can be more dramatic. A couple of weeks ago, the seedheads of the grasses were still full and a golden blond. Gaily offset against this background, there grew among them a spindly weed with a violet flower of four dainty petals. Today, the lanky weed towers above the frayed grasses, and, where its petals once were, the calyx has swollen and opened to yield a bright yellow thistle-like flower. The calyx itself has produced spiny spikes all around its surface, and is now a formidable cocklebur. One would not believe that the same stem recently bore the fragile violet flower, save that a few remain among them for testimony.

Man measures change, with such benchmarks as "sunrise" versus "sunset", and we refer to this measure as time. We arbitrarily say that "four weeks ago" there were violet flowers, "today" there are only cockleburs.

Measurement is comparison, and comparison is a willful act of choice. For those who have forsaken the habit of subjective comparison, time loses its relevance.

What is the importance of time to that ground squirrel who has scampered out of the brush and now bends a stalk of grass to lunch randomly among its seeds?

Time is the scaffolding upon which our sense of self rests for support. It is commonly accepted that that which I call my self was born on a particular day and will die on a particular day. And during its supposed existence, this self will be able to identify itself only in comparison—in contrast—to all that with which it interacts. We fail to see that while the cocklebur and the violet flower are *different*, their real *identity* is the same.

The Black Period

It has been a cloudy day throughout, and the night sky is overcast so that even the stars are not visible. I sit in a deck chair on the pool patio, across from two graceful date palms which are each lit from beneath. A few score feet away, a windchime reflects the gentle breeze which plays lightly across the pool's surface.

The pool is white with blue-tile trim, and an underwater light at each end provides pacific shades of undulating color, ranging from white through aquamarine to shadowy blue. This light, and the light reflected by the lacy palm fronds, attracts a few small moths who find themselves unable to break the water's surface tension to depart.

Cleo, one of the campground cats, comes for her evening inspection of the pool, stepping lithely through the narrow opening between two of the bars in the wrought-iron fence. She walks along the pool edge, stopping occasionally to study one of the moths fluttering on the water surface. She takes a place near a lounge chair across the pool from me, and, like me, contemplates the restful, transparent water. Soon, she leaves in the same manner she arrived.

A small frog leaps into the pool, so far from the edge that it appears to have fallen from the sky. There is enough chlorine in the water that one can detect it on the breeze; the frog swims swiftly to one side of the pool, but there is no side on which it could find easy access out.

A campground resident visits, via his golf cart, the nearby Coke machine. His boy, meanwhile, wanders over to the pool edge, notices the frog, scoops it out of the water with his hands, and releases it on the concrete. The frog jumps back into the water, sending a tiny ripple to both ends of the pool.

Poet Robert Bly has promulgated an instructive analogy. Three colors predominate most universally in primitive cultures, he observed, both in ornamentation and allusive description: white, black and red.

White seems typically to be associated with purity, innocence and youth (e.g., Snow White).

Red has been archetypal of passion; excitement, vigor, lust—the hottest of the colors, the color of blood.

Black is commonly associated with death, the void, the silence of the night, the priestly robes.

Their order in the natural course of life—allegorically in fable, poem or song—has suggested a "white period" from birth to adulthood, a "red period" of family and career activity through midlife, and a period of blackening, banked embers as the heat of physical life subsides.

However, given the relativity of what we refer to as time, there is not in every life an identical chronology. Nor are the distinctions so conveniently, as we say, black and white; while these colorations are different, they are—as are all things—in no way separate: all are forms of the same colorful energy. And, of course, no color has a higher ranking, or is consistently more appropriate, than the others.

Given this analogy, one may plunge from one period, or color, into another in an instant: from virgin to expectant mother; from high school graduate to bridegroom; and so on.

One may transit, by an unexpected divorce, from the red period of family responsibilities and business pursuits, to the black period of freedom from obligations and to introspection in spiritual inquiry.

One may also cross the black threshold through the sudden death of the self: the profound recognition that the separate self is an illusion; and that there is but the impenetrable void in which all and nothing are the same.

The questions which surface in the mind, during its black phase—the questions that revolve around "Who am I?"—are often present in the red or white phase, but as fruit yet to drop from the tree: the conditions, the order in a person's life, are not conducive to resolution. The black period is characterized by an end to personal ambition, to the psychological absence of a future, to an ending of time and all that it implies. This can occur at any instant in one's life, simultaneous with the realization of one's true identity.

The Beat Goes On

These little brown ants have finished their siesta of some one and a half hours, which began about noon. It's shadier and cooler now. The tentacle has reached out again from the handful of mounded sand that surrounds the entry to their earthen village, and it stretches north to south along the path's edge. They follow one fallen stalk of grass after another on a microcosmic single-lane freeway. At any given moment, there are about six moving bodies per inch of route, and the route stretches for five or six feet before you lose sight of it from your chair. Given their tiny, relative size this must be a foot journey of many miles in each direction. They are travelling fast enough that it is difficult to follow any particular individual by eye, and so each ant presumably travels many roundtrips per day; none of them appear, from here, to be overweight. You cannot discern that they are carrying any cargo in either direction; these hundreds of commuters are continually encountering one another head on, along a wire-thin stalk of grass, sometimes climbing over each other; given their speed, we humans would doubtless find this cursingly stressful.

You cannot help but wonder what is the source of the direction for their ordered, cooperative and coordinated behavior. Their communal energy is directed to, and from, the cool and dark subterranean mecca, and you would like to be able to look down in there and try to possibly make sense of what is going on. But you could not, even with delicate scientific instruments, unearth and cross-section this community and expect that its organic mysterium would meanwhile remain intact. Unfortunately, when man observes, man inevitably affects that which is observed.

There is, in truth, no observer which can be apart or disconnected from that which is observed. For as long as we view the mystery of existence as a question which can be posed and answered by the questioner, as subject to object, we cannot be one with, or wholly involved, in the question. Asking "Who am I?" is to irreparably sever the "I" from the "Who". There is no "I", there is no "Who", there is only being. The "Who" does not issue forth the "I", and the "I" does not return to the "Who". That consciousness which we know as a fragment—the personal self—can never know the consciousness which is wholly unfragmented, or "universal"…the consciousness which transcends individuated intelligence and is your true self and that of the ant.

The activity of the self, primarily, is accumulation. The self accumulates, basically, through memory. Therefore, the self is greedy for experience, particularly for enrichment, improvement, expansion.

When we sit contemplatively, or meditate, if there is even the faintest trace of ends/means, cause/effect, subject/object perspective, the self is both donor and beneficiary of the motivation. Stillness is not a means to betterment; were it a means to anything, it would be a means to the end of the self. To empty the self is not to better the self; it is to recognize that whose nature is change cannot be improved upon.

The key is attention to the moment, in such a way that *past* and *future* are not seen (and not seen, do not exist). In this manner, there is no consciousness of improvement for the self, there is no dissatisfaction with the present reality—since there is nothing which it is being compared to.

When there is no future which we are grasping for, there is no motivation for greed, nothing to be anticipated in fear.

Yet to make attention to the moment a discipline, a concerted effort, is to distract attention from the moment. To be alert does not suggest being in control; in attention, we are alert to our attentiveness and to our inattentiveness.

In activity, we concentrate; in attention, we are still. Stillness is not a means of improvement for the self. Stillness does not depend upon time for completion. Stillness is not a matter of control, but of order. The first item of order is to recognize your true identity; this can be seen in stillness. Attention to the moment is recognition of your self, and that energy which we call change.

Nothing Special

There is now a refined version of "Virtual Reality." After you settle in your chair, there are no switches to fiddle with. There is no glare from the screen. There's no color distortion. The scene which you are monitoring wraps entirely around you. That path that you view in front of you, you can actually feel it under your feet. Those little white flowers toward the forefront, you can breathe their herbal scent. You can actually feel on your shoulders the same breeze which ruffles the oak leaves, to the center left of the picture. And you can hear behind you, that jay which just flew out of vision. If you wish to, you can even get up, go over and look down into that snake hole without awaiting a close-up.

This not only gives you the truest picture of reality that it will be possible to get, it puts you right into it. That lizard that you were watching, chasing its tail, has now brushed against your foot.

We think in terms of going out to an untamed placed and "doing something." Any quiet spot in the woods or countryside is viewed as a testing ground for our skills—as hunter, camper, fisherman or whatever—an arena in which to contrast man's spirit to that of nature's, and to dominate. We do not consider going out into the wild, disturbing as little as possible along the way, and doing nothing.

Can you sit somewhere—anywhere—for, say, four hours and do nothing—without waiting for the time to end, without restlessness and boredom, without anxiety, regret or guilt? Can you sit quietly without an idea that you are, or need to be, "meditating", without counting the hours as merit bars in your "spiritual practice"?

With all of man's labor-saving devices, such as the computer, how many of us can experience the freedom of doing nothing, for no reason…not as another experience to be added to our trophies of experience, but as an end to the drive for experience? Stillness is both means and end, and more.

For hundreds of years, mystics have stressed the urgency of a "practice" which features the daily sitting of meditation. Those who follow this admonition must put their lives in order in such a way as to accommodate the requirements of devoted meditation. For those who shape their lives to facilitate daily meditation, half of their worldly problems have already been resolved by the time they sit down to mediate. The other half of their worldly concerns will be resolved only when they have paused to interface the mind with the self.

Freedom is not at the end of this process, as a product; freedom is the process. To free oneself for a contemplative life is to free oneself from convention. One has reorganized one's priorities, and they are no longer the typical priorities.

To "sit quietly, doing nothing" is to sit without awaiting or expecting anything—such as a "result" from the activity. Freeing oneself from the cause/effect perspective is a part of the freeing process. Freeing oneself from the idea that anything in particular "should" happen, "ought" to happen, "must" happen, is part of the process which frees one from the chains of time, even as one sits.

To "sit quietly, doing nothing" means that nothing else need be done: *just sit*, quietly. The freedom to do nothing is freedom.

As Is

The sun has burned away the cloud layer, by this late afternoon, and is now behind and to the side of me.

Earlier, a mature squirrel came down the path in front of me, to within a couple of dozen inches of my feet, before pausing for a long, blank look at me and then returning the way it came.

Now, one of the lizards has sought the slim crescent of shade provided under the arch of my foot, with even its long tail tucked away out of sight.

I am marveling at a grasshopper, among the dried grass and leaves off to one side of my chair. It is about an inch long, but, sitting as quietly as it is, one could peruse the ground for many minutes before discovering it—so effective is its camouflage coloration.

Somehow, the lizard has noticed it too, and darts away to pounce on and seize it. The grasshopper is fully one-tenth as large as the entire lizard, tail included, and it manages to set its feet to earth and spring away from the lizard's jaws. The lizard swiftly pounces again, and, as quickly, the grasshopper leaps away again. And so they go, down the path, until the grasshopper jumps far into the grass on the embankment, where the lizard cannot easily see.

·

Between you and I stands my past image, creating a space/time relationship between us…as would a hurdle which we needed to cross in order to embrace. This image is formed by speculative thought: such things as belief, prejudice, memory, expectation, desire, etc.

When we can look at others without the interference of image, we can look at relationship—to all things, even to "God"—without the mediation of image, without preconceived and limited conceptions.

When one has perceived without images and symbols and forms, what has become of thoughts, words and ideas (such as "I" and "others") which are representative images?

"I" am a montage of past images, and that montage of images attempts to examine "itself"—collated past images.

The I which attempts to compare and improve upon myself is the I which sets itself apart from you.

To "have an attitude" means to take a position, and to take a position implies inflexibility, defensiveness. The attitude is predicated on past experience and assumption of future behavior. One takes a position in preparation to react.

The present embodies unlimited potential for change; expectation is a hinderance, a detraction, here. Conditions change from minute to minute: how could we even form an appropriate attitude in this moment unless we abandoned every previous attitude?

It is outdated attitudes and conditioned, knee-jerk reactions which are a cause of anguish for each generation, and, implicitly, for each calcified individual.

Our position is continually challenged and our guard is constantly up, a situation of unceasing tension.

Rigidity is the characteristic of rigor mortis. There are no new discoveries in a dead mind. No possibilities are closed to an open mind.

Transit

These summer days are unarguably peaceful. It is too warm, apparently, for the bothersome little black flies, even in the shade. The ants, as well, seem touched by lethargy. The lizard doesn't leave its burrow until nearly a couple of hours after noon.

The vegetation on the hill is nearly as brown as green, and the only blossoms of color are a tough cottony white; when these blossoms dry, they oxidize to the color of rust. Finches sway on the stalks of a shrub, eating seeds where there once were flowers.

To evade, to struggle, is to deny the reality of this moment. To resist is to attempt to forestall until some future, "better" development.

The bees find less to attract them now; the droning background hum is gone. A bee alights on the cookie in my left hand, and approves of the raisins. It then cautiously hovers over my thermos cup, walks delicately on the rim, and samples a brown drop of coffee. It does not approve.

The birds have suspended their cooing, mating and nesting, and an occasional broken eggshell is all that remains to be seen of their romance.

To resist is to maintain a subject/object relationship to that which is resisted. Struggle is a "gaining" idea. Evasion is ambitious.

The yellow-and-black butterfly has passed through for the day, and it is time for the two tiger-orange butterflies to tie endless bows in the air. The weeds gossip amiably among themselves in the breeze, and this is carried to the shrubs on the embankment, and then it moves the oak trees aflutter.

Dishonesty is resistance to truth, to the 'what is'. Resistance is the expression of fear.

The sky is a flat pastel backdrop, highlighting those earthly colors, such as the metallic black raven, which are contrasted against it. It gives not a hint that countless glimmering stars are hidden away in it, soon to be displayed with the unfolding of night.

Live It

Sensible only is one thing: to live day by day, moment to moment. It is not that all will take care of itself (though it will); it's that you cannot control conditions which do not actually yet exist.

The "worst" which any future could hold is the emptiness of death, and that condition is inseparable from emptiness in life.

But he cannot live from day to day who is driven by desire, pursuit of pleasure and attachment to security.

When you recognize your true self, desire ends. With the ending of desire, there is no need for time. Where there is no time, there remains but the moment which is.

One recognizes it in an instant; to live it is a lifetime.

Can you relax somewhere comfortably, with no plan, no agenda, no timetable, and with no trace of desire to be in any other place or to do any other thing? Can you be free entirely of the sense of awaiting anything whatsoever? Can you die peacefully and lastingly into the moment of eternity? That is the moment, the limitless moment, where there is freedom from mortal fear.

You will not find yourself in this relaxed position until there is a natural order in your life. And you will not be open to the unfolding of this order until you perceive unequivocally the implications of your true identity.

The truth of your identity is to be found in solitude…stillness…emptiness. It is to be found in the moment from which nothing is separable.

To be able to sit for hours without wanting anything special or needing anything—without wanting to do anything or needing to do anything—

is a remarkable freedom. To not be driven by the ego, by a feeling of incompleteness, is a peace that surpasseth understanding. To feel the security of invulnerability to insecurity is a blessing. To be unenthralled by time, as distance between self and non-self as death, is liberating.

Being as free as a bird can mean to be free to perch unhurriedly, as well as to fly. Where need one go, in the search for peace? Freedom is not at the end of a road, it is not an accomplishment. To sit down and shut up is an unacknowledged virtue.

You are primal energy's capacity to view the vibrant colors which are an extension of primal energy.

You are primal energy's capacity to audit the birdsong which is an expression of primal energy.

You are the nose of the unconfined energy which appreciates the unconfined scent of the flowers.

You are nature's tongue which savors the delectable melons of nature.

You are the flesh of the universe which revels in the hot sun of the universe.

You are the sense of life. And you are the awareness that you are that sense.

You are energy sensing yourself, and you are not in any way separate from that which is sensed.

The sense, the sensing and the sensed are one.

There is, in the movement of energy, only the sensing; and, in that, is the sensing of change.

You are the change you sense.

Robert Wolfe
www.livingnonduality.org

write Robert c/o
Karina Library Press
PO Box 35, Ojai CA 93024
or
robert@livingnonduality.org

Share this book with others:
elementarycloudwatching.com

Would you like to leave a review?
elementarycloudwatching.com/review

CPSIA information can be obtained
at www.ICGtesting.com
Printed in the USA
LVHW061503190323
741975LV00006B/283